A Deaf Dog Joins the Family

A Deaf Dog Joins the Family

TRAINING, EDUCATION, AND COMMUNICATION
FOR A SMOOTH TRANSITION

Terrie Hayward

ISBN: 1507578261
ISBN 13: 9781507578261

This book is dedicated to all of the special people who have opened their homes to dogs who hear with their hearts.

And to Jo Ann Sosa & Milena Massey who rescued our deaf dog, Blanca from the abandoned gas station in Isabella, Puerto Rico.

Contents

Acknowledgements

Thanks to:
Mark Hayward for accepting Blanca as another furry family member.

Friends & family who reviewed earlier versions of the book & helped me along the way.

The many deaf dog families who responded overwhelmingly with wonderful photo submissions of their deaf pups.

Also to Deaf Dogs Rock, The Deaf Dog Network, & My Deaf Dog groups for their support of deaf dogs globally!

About the Author

Terrie Hayward holds a Master's Degree in Bilingual Special Education, is a Karen Pryor Academy, Certified Training Partner, and holds a CPDT-KA (Council of Professional Dog Trainers-Knowledge Assessed) certification.

She continues to pursue ongoing professional development opportunities as well including the Professional Animal Training Seminar with Ken Ramirez, Contemporary Animal Training and Management, at NEI, the Living and Learning with Animals for Professionals certificate course, Behavior Works, and Canine Behavioral Evaluation Workshop, Animal Alliance.

She has worked in the rescue realm for over twenty years whilst living in Papua New Guinea, Samoa, the British Virgin Islands, and Puerto Rico. Terrie wanted to combine her background in education and training with her passion to enable her to positively effect change in animal's lives. She went back to school to become a professional, certified, positive reinforcement animal trainer and continues to learn and grow via working with people and animals.

Although previously, Terrie had never considered science one of her favorite fields, she has since discovered and concluded that the science of behavior is amazing and awe-inspiring. She has enjoyed continuing her education via many professional development opportunities, which include working with macaws at Natural Encounters, Inc., training chickens at Legacy Canine, and beluga whales at Shedd Aquarium.

Terrie works to use the least intrusive, most effective educational alternatives available. In doing so she empowers animals and people towards better communication and more confident, comfortable lives. She loves the fact that science ties all learners together and that via positive reinforcement training and the understanding of how the science of behavior functions she can work to improve lives of the animals and the caregivers that she collaborates with.

Thus, with her business, PAW-Positive Animal Wellness, she is pleased to make improving the lives, care, teaching, and learning of animals and people her career.

Additional information about Terrie and PAW can be found on her website at: www.positiveanimalwellness.com

Blanca

Blanca 2015

n 2013, a friend named Milena had recently rescued a large, but skeletal dog from an abandoned gas station. She'd contacted me for some possible training help. The dog, who had 10 puppies the very day following her rescue, was big, strong, and exuberant. I'd agreed to go by and to help to evaluate and to do some training with the mom, while assisting with puppy duty.

Although I had fostered, adopted, and cared for hundreds of dogs I had yet to have met a deaf dog in my personal or professional life.

With her all white coat, my friend named this dog, Blanca (meaning "white" in Spanish). Blanca responded eagerly to attention and appeared motivated to figure out how to earn small pieces of hotdog. Always armed with my treat pouch and clicker, I was ready to mark (with a click) and reinforce (with hotdog) behavior that I liked. I ignored her jumping and reinforced with a click and then some cheese for her sit. We moved around and repeated the behavior. My friend then mentioned that she thought that the dog might have trouble hearing and wondered if she was just responding to my body language. Milena had come to this conclusion as she said that in the early morning she could easily come right up to Blanca without her even stirring. Blanca seemed to ignore the hungry cries of her puppies. We also noted that while other dogs barked, or car horns honked, Blanca remained seemingly unaware.

It was a few visits later when we determined after various sound tests, that Blanca was in fact deaf. As I had never encountered this before, I started to do some research on deafness in dogs.

At first it came as a surprise to me that in many cases in the past, and perhaps even, sadly nowadays, deafness would be an immediate reason to put a dog to sleep. It was increasingly shocking to me over time as I watched this intelligent, loving dog learn, that her lack of hearing could have meant her instant death. While her deafness is a bit of an alternative training challenge and requires some modifications, I believe that her other senses (smell, peripheral vision, body language) may actually be enhanced, as often happens when humans are deaf. Although all dogs are very acutely aware of body language, deaf dogs (I believe certainly true in Blanca's case) are perhaps even more keenly observant of body language and gestures.

In fact, deaf dogs may require that families focus on training the way that we certainly can for all dogs, but don't as folks rely on verbal (often not entirely effectual) communication to suffice. Deaf dogs can teach us a lot about care, compassion, and training methods, and Blanca seems ever so joyful and eager to learn and respond now that someone has taken the time to learn how to communicate with her!

Deafness and the Basics of Living With a Deaf Dog

Canine deafness can be temporary or permanent and it can be congenital or acquired.

The AKC Canine Health Foundations states "Deafness, in dogs as in people, is the inability to hear. Deafness can be unilateral (affecting one ear) or bilateral (affecting both ears)."

Causes of Deafness

Scott Vinnicomb
Photography, Radar

There are two types of deafness: congenital (which means existing at birth) and acquired (AKC Canine Health Foundation, definitions to follow).

Congenital Deafness: Some dogs are born without the ability to hear due to developmental defects in the hearing apparatus. Deafness can develop in the first few weeks of life when the ear canal is still closed and occurs when the blood supply to the cochlea degenerates and the nerve cells die. Congenital deafness in dogs is permanent.

Interestingly, it is usually linked to a defective gene and is inherited. Often the defective gene is for coat color. Dogs with white or merle coats are predisposed to congenital deafness. Most of the dog breeds that suffer from congenital deafness have some white pigmentation in their coats.

More specifically, according to George M. Strain, Professor of Neuroscience, Louisiana State University, although researchers still aren't sure what causes congenital deafness, they do know it's most common in dogs with white or nearly white heads. "The lack of pigment on the head causes the pigment cells in the inner ear to fail to develop, or they may be lacking entirely," Strain says. "The lack of pigment cells causes the death of the nerve cells that need to develop for hearing to occur."

There are approximately 85 dog breeds with reported congenital deafness. Some of these breeds are more susceptible to deafness than others, with high prevalence in the Australian Cattle Dog, the Australian Shepherd, the Bull Terrier, the Catahoula Leopard Dog, the Dalmatian, the English Cocker Spaniel and the English Setter.

Acquired Deafness: Dogs with acquired deafness are born with the capability of developing and maintaining normal hearing, but hearing is lost. Some dogs with acquired deafness have only partial hearing loss that may not be noticeable to the owner. Others have severe hearing loss. Acquired deafness is not common to any one breed and is usually the result of damage to the ear components such as the eardrum, middle or inner ear structures, and nerves.

Diseases, such as canine distemper can be the root cause of ear damage. Some other causes of hearing loss include excessive amounts of wax, dirt, hair or other material plugging the ear canal; inflammation of the ear canal; untreated infections of the middle (otitis externa) or internal ear (otitis interna); a torn or ruptured ear drum; loud noise; head trauma; ear mites and old age.

In addition, certain drugs, often used to treat life-threatening infections in dogs can cause ototoxicity or disturbances in hearing and/or balance.

Diagnosing Deafness

While your veterinarian can initially examine your dog's ears and in more serious cases a procedure called BAER (Brainstem Auditory Evoked Response) may be conducted, a less scientific test can be conducted at home by making a loud sound -such as clapping hands- behind your dog whilst they are sleeping or not looking at you and while they are unaware of your position. You'll want to be certain that you aren't close enough for them to feel the vibrations, which would provide inaccurate test results. Deaf dogs often appear to be sleeping incredibly deeply. They also may have a lack of response of any kind to doorbells, horns, or other sudden loud sounds. They might startle easily when approached unawares, and may seem confused or unresponsive to vocal cues.

Communication

Morag Heirs, Ph.D. Well Connected Canine, Farah

Finding out that your dog is deaf does not mean that you are unable to communicate effectively with your pup. With some slight modifications and the patience and consistency that is vitally important to working with any animal, you and your dog can easily make great progress towards understanding each other.

Too, it is still important and helpful to speak with your deaf dog as they, again, are keenly aware of body language cues.

Language

The absence of a verbal language, while, at first seemingly intimidating to some humans, is often not at all problematic for dogs who are intensely aware of subtle communications via body language. Body language reading is a well developed skill for most dogs. Think of a time when you glanced at the leash inadvertently while wondering if you should take your dog out for a walk. Meanwhile, your dog has raced to the door and is waiting. This is an example of body language communication! In an excerpt from Through A Dog's Eyes by Jennifer Arnold, "Evolutionary anthropologist Brian Hare speculates that the ability to read human body language was one of the traits selected when dogs were being domesticated. In other words, dogs that were better at reading people were more likely to be nurtured by humans and, therefore, have the opportunity to successfully reproduce."

Since you won't be using a verbal language with your dog you will need to develop some visual cues. Again, as dogs are very aware of human body language, visual cues will be a concept which is already occurring without effort, whether you're aware of it or not.

We will, however, choose distinct visual cues to signify specific vocabulary (such as "car" or "food") or behaviors (like "sit," "lie down," and "look at me") that we can use to communicate with our deaf dogs.

While dogs are very good at figuring out body language and thus visual cues, we once more will want to make things as easy as possible for our dogs to understand. Hence, once we choose a cue for a specific word or behavior, while it is possible to have more than one cue and even to change them, initially, it will be best for the clearest communication to be as consistent as possible. This means, choosing one visual cue per word or behavior. Do the cue the same way each time. Have everyone giving the cue also do the cue the same way each time. This seemingly sounds like an obvious statement, however, subtle differences can make cues confusing. Thus, practicing (without your deaf dog) and deciding as a family on consistent cue delivery will help your dog to understand more quickly and easily.

Attention

Vanessa L. Smith, Rufus

Getting your deaf dog's attention is another consideration as it will not be possible to call out to your pup. Fostering a "check in" behavior, which we talk about more in the training section, is key. Each and every time that your dog looks at you, you will want to signal that this a good thing and reinforce this behavior.

You can also sometimes get your deaf dog's attention via vibrations. Tapping or stomping on the floor may make enough of a vibration to attract your dog's attention. Once he looks at you, you can then signal (mark) and reinforce that attention.

Additionally, waving hands or arms at a distance can gain your dog's interest. Again once he looks in your direction mark and reinforce that attention to you!

If it's dark or dusk you can flick the lights off and on to draw your dog's attention back to you.

Some people may use a small flashlight, however remember to never shine the light directly into the dog's eyes, nor is it advisable to use a laser pointer. You would use the flashlight like a "clicker" or a special signal and turn it on/off quickly to mark a behavior. Remember that every time you mark you will want to follow up with something that your dog find's reinforcing. The marker is like a "promise" of access earned to something reinforcing, so be sure to keep your promises by providing that access after each marker.

You might also work on training a shoulder tap to mean "look at me." Tap your dog on the shoulder and then pop something yummy (just a tiny piece) in their mouth. Repeat this often and in every room of your home and then begin to practice this outside as well. Your dog will come to understand that the tap equals good things for him and will begin to turn back to you anticipating the yummy treat. Continue to practice and "pay" for him turning to look at you. Eventually, after many, many, many repetitions, you can sometimes replace your reinforcer (the yummy treat) with some patting/love. In order to keep the behavior strong once it has been established (i.e. once your dog turns to look at you when you tap him on the shoulder) you will still want to surprise your dog from time to time with something delicious as a reward.

When moving from room to room around your house it is nice if you can let your deaf dog know that you've gone. Walking past them or a light touch on your way out may help them to feel less anxious if they've been able to see you go. They may choose to follow you or to stay put, however, the anxiety of not knowing what happened to you has been eliminated.

Sleeping

Kathi Hiatt, Odd Otis

Deaf dogs can easily startle when awakened. You might try putting a tiny, tasty piece of treat (sardines, for example have a strong smell) in front of your dog's nose. This way, when they awaken, it will be to something positive that they enjoy. You can also gently touch your deaf dog to awaken them; however, be careful never to allow children to bother a sleeping dog, deaf or hearing.

Startle Response

Cheyenne Fogarty, Felony

Deaf dogs often startle. As they are unable to hear an approach, and sometimes nor can they feel vibrations of someone nearing, they may startle when you suddenly appear. It is a good idea to begin working on associating people's approach with positive things. You may have a tiny bit of a yummy food each time you get near your deaf dog. You might also want to begin conditioning them to a tap near the hind quarters which, when they turn results in something positive (again, a small piece of some very desirable food, and later an appreciative pet or scratch behind the ears).

Safety

Judy Small, Chance

With a deaf dog, it is important to consider and follow through with some safety precautions. Blanca wears a harness with a "deaf dog" velcro sign (purchased on Amazon.com). This way, in the unlikely event of her escape, folks would understand her lack of response to shouts and other noises.

It is also very important to not have your deaf dog off leash, except in a securely fenced area as your deaf pup will obviously not be able to hear traffic sounds and/or you calling him/her if lost. There should be few exceptions to this rule. In rare situations, there are individuals who have trained a fail-proof "sit" or "down stay" cue and may allow their dog off leash in certain unfenced areas. However, most people won't have that training in place and as such, the safest spot is in a completely fenced yard and even then, supervision is still best to avoid any possible escapes or harm coming to your dog in the yard alone.

The other reasonable choice is to use a long, cloth leash. Retractable leashes are popular nowadays, but have many dangers associated (leash burns, cuts, amputation, lack of control) and thus aren't something I advocate. Dogs can have lots of fun and fulfilling lives without being unsafely unleashed. Long walks, short, but interesting strolls, and positive reinforcement training all offer mental and physical stimulation to keep your pup happy and well.

PAW Positive Animal Wellness, Jax

Finally, you may consider placing a little bell on her collar. This way, if she's loose (even in the house or a fenced area), you can hear her movement whilst she's unable to respond to your calls.

As with any dog, micro chipping and identification tags with current contact information (keeping it up to date after moves or phone number changes is key) are important safety features for your pet.

Welcoming a Deaf Dog Into Your Home

Welcoming your new dog into your home is an exciting time! There are a few items to have on hand and some tips that I share below that will make sure the transition is smooth for the dog and your household.

You will want to have:

- an appropriately sized crate (see CRATE TRAINING for types of crates and training how to's)
- a flat buckle collar (best for identification, however harnesses are best for walking as they don't pull on delicate necks)
- a harness (Easy Walk or Balance Harness are some recommended options)
- a leash (6-8 ft flat, cloth leash and perhaps a longer line-again, NOT a retractable one)
- a water bowl
- food bowl and food puzzles (see CONTRA FREELOADING section for explanation and ideas)

Belle & Jason Kemmis, Lottie

- toys and appropriate items to chew on (Nylar bones, stuffed toys, rope bones, KONGS and other food puzzles-always used with supervision at the beginning)
- a bed (that fits in crate is a good idea)
- dog shampoo (if you plan on some DIY bathing)
- healthy, nutritious food and treats

Next are some resources that will help you in welcoming this new pup into your home.. In addition to what you are reading right now, you may want to consult with a positive reinforcement trainer. I offer distance coaching/training/consulting-more information can be found at www.positiveanimalwellness.com. Having a few sessions with a professional may help you and your dog to feel more confident and comfortable. Plus, it is a great bonding experience

The Pet Professional Guild http://www.petprofessionalguild.com/PetGuildMembers or Karen Pryor Academy https://www.karenpryoracademy.com/find-a-trainer both have listings of force free trainers which can be located by zip code or country.

Consulting a trainer at the very beginning of your journey with your new dog is highly recommended as it helps set you up for success. Training behaviors correctly from the start is much easier than attempting to "correct" issues after they have been practiced and reinforced. Try to begin by being as prepared as possible and as patient as you can. Break training into very small bits and times; training sessions should occur multiple times per day, but be no longer than 1-3 minutes per session. Repetition is key and patience will get you there!

While you can make up any cues and signs that you like for working with your dog, a spot to begin is by using some American Sign Language signs (ASL). This site allows you to type in a word and view a short video of the ASL: http://www.handspeak.com. Making some modifications to some of the ASL signs may be helpful as some require two hands and sometimes you may only have one hand available.

Establishing a consistent routine will help your new dog to predict what happens and when which can be comforting. Remember that patience and consistency will set you and your deaf dog up for success!

Training

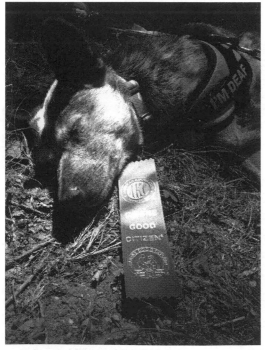
Kirsten Westerfeld, Quinn

As mentioned earlier in the book, I am a positive reinforcement trainer. Training via modern, science-based methods is the most effective and ethical route to communicating with your dog. According to expert trainer Ken Ramirez, "Teaching animals how to live in our world is a shared process. The student needs to want to learn and it should be a fun partnership. Training is a natural process!"

According to Bob McMillan, "Force free is a philosophy, not an ad slogan. Mixing any other training style with positive training is like your neighborhood vegetarian cafe adding an all-you-can-eat steak night on Thursdays to boost traffic. It's simply incompatible." That is to say, training is such an integral and important part of your relationship with your dog that using positive reinforcement is the best way to improve your communication.

Ken Ramirez, world-renowned animal behavior expert also asserts that there are four cornerstones to animal care: nutrition, veterinary care, environment (including social environment), and training (and enrichment). These four pieces must be in place for the welfare of your dog and for their best chance at a flourishing and fulfilling life.

Positive reinforcement training is comprised of three components: observation (watching for the behavior), marking (signaling that that specific behavior was the one that we wanted), and reinforcing (providing something that the learner considers reinforcing which will increase the likelihood of that behavior being repeated).

When marking a behavior with hearing dogs, we would often use a verbal marker (like the word, "yes!") or a small device called a "clicker". The timing of your marker is very important, as it indicates to the dog the specific behavior that we liked and will want to see again. With a deaf dog, an auditory marker won't work, so we have to use a visual signal. In Blanca's case we use an open hand "flash" (fist closed and all fingers "flick" quickly open). That signal tells her "Yes! That thing that you JUST did is the exact behavior that has earned you an opportunity for something that you find reinforcing."

Next, we will want to follow up our marker with something that the dog finds reinforcing. This means that we need to put ourselves in the mind of our dog. Although, you might consider a pat on the head to be something of a great reinforcer for your dog, your dog may think that it's about a 1 on a scale of 1-10 (with 10 being the top of the chart!). Taking a moment to find "level 10" reinforcers specific to your dog will be the first step. Foods, which to many dogs constitute high-value reinforcers, may include the following: chicken, hotdogs, cheese, steak, ham, liver, peanut butter, and spray cheese. Lower value reinforcers normally include dry kibble and store-bought treats. Reinforcers may also be environmental-from getting to go for a walk to riding in the car or going through a gate to the yard where they can play outside. There can also be be toys as well as affection. However, using food (something highly palatable to your dog) is small, easily deliverable, fast (so that you can get in many repetitions, instead of, for example, waiting for a ball to be returned to you) and a primary reinforcer (in that your dog has to eat to live).

A List of Reinforcers

Food: hot dogs, cheerios, chicken, cheese, boiled egg, sardines, tuna, sausage bits, steak, ham, spray cheese, commercial dog treats, dry dog food, peanut butter, baby food, cream cheese, bacon.

Note: If using dry food, you can mix it in with other training treats so that the dry food soaks up some of the flavor and scent. You can also reduce the amount at meal time by what you might be using for training if you are concerned about weight management or intestinal issues.

Environmental: attention, praise, being around people (or dogs, cats, birds, other animals), running, jumping, playing, swimming, going outside, coming inside, going for a car ride, jumping on the bed/couch, toys, children, bicycles.

There is a great book all about motivation for your animal written by fellow trainers Deb Jones and Denise Fenzi. It is available here: http://www.thedogathlete.com/collections/books

Remember, the animal is the one who chooses what they find reinforcing. So, even if you might believe that love from you or a store bought dog biscuit is a level 10," you may need to do some experimentation to see just what your dog is most eager to work for.

Scott Vinnicombe Photography, Radar

Also, do keep in mind that reinforcers may change contextually. In other words, while your dog may be perfectly interested in working for some kibble at home, in the park with distractions such as other animals, people, sounds, and smells, you may require a higher value reinforcer for your dog to respond to cues.

Punishment vs Reinforcement

Rather than waiting for your dog to do something that you don't like and then punishing them for it (which they may or may not understand correlates to the behavior that you are seeking to curtail), instead, set dogs up for success! Manage while training so that your dog doesn't have the opportunity to do things that you don't want repeated. Use crates and baby gates and tethering and keep your eyes on your pup. Pick up things that you don't want them to chew and provide safe, appropriate alternatives.

Frequently folks may not realize the negative impact that aversives can have on behavior. When it comes to training, the biggest issue is that punishment, discipline, and corrections can lead to aggression, apathy, generalized fear, and escape/avoidance behaviors. This isn't a list of things that most folks want for their companion animals. Such techniques as water sprays, grabbing neck scruff, yelling, "schhtt sounds," shouting "No!," leash corrections, force release of items, or staring down threateningly can all have very negative consequences.

Aggression can be the result of aversive techniques as learners become frightened and frustrated. Apathy may be the result of punishment as learners realize that "it's just no use" and thus shut down to all learning. Generalized fear is a potential side effect of corrections as learners might always be frightened of "men" or "people wearing hats" based upon interactions with the people imparting the corrections. Finally, escape-avoidance may come about as a result of discipline techniques as the learner learns to fear and attempt to avoid the person with whom they regularly associate punishment.

To help get your head wrapped around the idea of reinforcement, try counting out fifty pieces of tiny delicious treats. By the day's end commit to using all 50 pieces to reinforce behaviors that you want to see repeated.

By using the "50 pieces" game above you will be switching from waiting for behaviors and punishing to watching for behaviors and reinforcing! Remember, that behaviors that are reinforced will be repeated. Often, when folks are intending to "punish" a behavior with words (shouting) or actions (physical corrections) they inadvertently reinforce behaviors with conversation and attention, which may be just what your dog is seeking. Instead, reinforce what you like and ignore what you don't. Better yet, ask for something that you DO like and then can reinforce when your dog does it instead.

A quick tip for how to use reinforcement when teaching your dog to respond to visual cues: When teaching a new sign don't try to introduce the sign by signing and asking for the behavior; rather, watch for the behavior (capture) and then "label" it with the sign so that your pup can understand the sign=the behavior.

Dealing with Frustration

Folks may often may feel as though the animal understands what they are attempting to communicate, but are simply choosing not to respond as desired.

In other instances, people experience frustration at difficulties in communicating the desired outcome to their dogs.

With a deaf dog, these feelings of exasperation may be intensified. Try to remember that even if you believe that you have broken down the task into very small, manageable pieces and are communicating very clearly and efficiently, you are in fact communicating with a different species.

Imagine for a moment that you were training your dog to place a red toy on top of a blue one. After your dog has seemingly mastered the behavior pretend that he has gotten it correct 100% of the time for two weeks straight. Then, one day, he places the blue toy on top of the red one. The issue is not stubbornness, nor defiance, but rather a problem of communication. Your dog may have thought all along that the correct behavior was to stack up the two toys. He may have coincidentally stacked red on blue for two weeks, thus leading you to believe that your training was clear. When, in fact there was a lack of clear communication and training.

Because humans are very verbally oriented via our information exchange, we may struggle without this means of communication with our pup. Thus, any time that you feel overwhelmed, stop, and take a break. Revert back to something very simple, like making eye contact and begin there. Celebrate tiny successes and remember that this is a marathon and not a sprint; your communication and training with your deaf pup, as with hearing dogs, will be a lifelong endeavor.

Try to keep in mind that learning is not an upward linear journey, but that there may be setbacks and confusion. Maintain a positive attitude, take pride in small milestones, and acknowledge that your relationship is becoming stronger. This is key to working successfully with your deaf dog.

How to Start Training Your Dog

In the case of training your deaf pup, I suggest starting with the basics (often different from what folks with experience in more traditional methods might suspect) with slight modifications.

The first step is that you want "looking at you" to be incredibly reinforcing for your dog. Animals, and all learners, by nature, will do what is most reinforcing. Thus, we need to have your deaf dog believe that looking at you is absolutely wonderful. With this, we are going to be fostering a "check in" behavior.

Lisa Chapin, Halie

Standing in front of your dog, when they look at you, use your "marker" hand signal and then provide something reinforcing (example, a tiny, tiny piece of chicken or hotdog). The size can be very small, as you are providing a reinforcer and not a meal. Also, we want to do many, many repetitions, which means many, many reinforcers, so the smaller the better to allow for repeats and for the dog not filling up.

As soon as your dog looks at you again, mark (use your hand signal) and then reinforce (deliver the treat)! The object is to "catch" your dog looking at you and mark and reinforce. Be prepared, because it will happen a lot. Carry a treat pouch (http://store.clickertraining.com/terry-ryan-treat-pouch.html) so that you are always ready, especially at the beginning. Tether your dog to you (leashed and attached to you) so that you make it easy to catch your dog looking at you. Set the situation up for success!

Michelle Langton, Romeo

A "check in" behavior is something that you want to foster early and often. Your deaf dog voluntarily "checking in" with you will make it easier for you to then communicate with them, which is even more important when they don't have their sense of hearing. Consistently looking at you, checking in with you, and looking to you for cues will aid greatly with communication.

Once you have found something(s) that your dog will consider worthwhile to work for (super reinforcing), and your dog understands (because you have repeatedly marked and reinforced that behavior) that looking at you is a very good thing, you want to condition that response with a cue.

Cues vs Commands

While you may be familiar with the term "command," the word "cue" might be a nebulous expression. The two words, however are not interchangeable. The difference is that whereby a command intimates an implied threat ("Do this or else…"), a cue offers the opportunity for access to something that the learner finds reinforcing (they get something that they like). The sky is the limit when it comes to deaf dogs learning cues.

Judy Small, Chance

The average pet owner may stop with the basic "sit," "down," and "stay" style communications, and/or by default, the hearing dog may learn "walk," "car," and "food." Deaf dog caregivers, on the other hand, will actively need to teach a cue for each of the behaviors/vocabulary that they want their dog to understand.

Folks may then pose the question as to what sign or signal will equal which cue. As mentioned earlier, some people like to use ASL-American Sign Language and some may already have some visual cues that they have taught dogs (like a downward hand motion to signal that it's time to lie down). The decision is up to you. I had a friend who needed to teach a new cue (to her hearing dog) for "sit." She decided on the word "spaghetti;" you may use whichever cue you think appropriate, as long as it's visual rather than auditory.

For your first sign, you will want to consider which visual cue you will use for your "yes" marker. Three of the most common ones are a "thumbs up" sign, a "hand flick" (fist closed then flicking open), or "clapping hands." Whichever one you pick you will need to be consistent.

You can then begin to associate that "yes" sign with something reinforcing. Do your "yes" sign and then give your dog a tiny piece of cheese. Repeat 10-15 times and do this 5 times per day for three days. Do your "yes" sign in many different places and follow with something reinforcing; your dog will quickly get that your "yes" sign means something good!

Next, catch your dog doing something that you like, such as looking at you. When your dog looks at you, use your "yes" sign and then reinforce! Be certain to reinforce each and every time that you mark as not doing so will weaken your marker. Your "clicker" or "yes" sign is like a promise. Always be true to your promises and reinforce each time you signal a marker!

Educate

You will frequently hear people talking about teaching your deaf dog a sign for "no." Just as with my hearing dogs, the word "no" holds no value. Often folks are encouraged to let dogs know that they are displeased or prefer that they don't continue with certain behaviors by saying the word, "no." The word, "no," however is one that you might consider eliminating entirely from your vocabulary with your pup.

The issue is that "no" doesn't tell the dog what exactly we don't want him to do. It doesn't let her know what we would like her to do. And, bonus, saying "no" actually may act as a reinforcer for the dog. When you say, "no" you are paying attention to your dog, you are speaking; or in the case of our deaf dogs, we are still communicating with facial cues and attentive body language, and often the word is exclaimed with great enthusiasm, which may seem exciting to your dog (again, with our deaf dogs, think facial expressions).

Instead, consider ignoring a behavior that you prefer not to see repeated. Without reinforcement, research shows that the behavior will extinguish. Furthermore, you can teach and put on cue an incompatible behavior. Just as you can't be in two places at once, you can't do two opposing things at the same time. An example of this would be teaching the dog to sit as sitting is incompatible with jumping.

Judy Small, Chance

Finally, catch your dog doing something right and praise and reward. After all, if you change your vocabulary to include more of the word, "yes" you will find you have a happier, healthier relationship with your pet.

So, instead of "no," I recommend teaching a nice default behavior, such as a hand target (more on hand targets to follow). That way, if your dog is doing something that you don't like, you can 1. Ignore it. The rule of thumb is to ignore what you don't like and reinforce what you do. 2. Ask for your default behavior, thus setting your dog up to succeed as you are then able to mark and reinforce your dog doing something that you DO like!

This is an activity to help you practice getting your mind set around seeking, marking, and reinforcing behavior that you like and would want your dog to repeat. Instead of feeding your dog in a bowl (a lost opportunity anyhow: http:// positiveanimalwellness.com/contrafreeloading-free-food-or-earned-food/), take the measured amount of daily kibble and distribute to family members. Explain to everyone that by the end of the day, your deaf dog needs to have gotten every piece of this kibble. Ask everyone to watch (observe) your dog and then mark (sign for "yes!") every time your dog is doing something that they like (sitting, laying down relaxing, not barking, looking at you, acting calm, following you, etc.). Be certain to follow up that marker with a reinforcer, in this case a piece of the dog's daily kibble! Watch how often you can catch your dog doing something that you like!

Often times people wait for their dog to fail and then correct or punish them. Instead, try to catch your dog in the act of doing something that you like and mark and reinforce it. Remember, behaviors that are reinforced are repeated and will grow stronger!

Default Behavior

A "default" behavior is a behavior that you will teach your dog that you will practice over and over so that it becomes something that they can do without much thought. It becomes a "default" as in, "When all else fails, I do this because it earns me something that I want." Default behaviors can become something that the dog is able to do when they are aroused or distracted or stressed.

A nice default behavior that you can teach your deaf dog is a "hand target." Targeting is a building block behavior and has great value. It is a focus behavior. It is also a behavior, which is incompatible; which means it can't be done simultaneously, with jumping, for example. Hand targeting is also incompatible with what may be described as acting "crazy," and it is a behavior which can be used as a "warm up" in new or distracting environments, or when your dog is unsettled. Once your dog knows how to target your hand you can eventually use it to move your dog from place to place without physical manipulation. For example, you can target your dog up into the car, down off of the couch, or onto the scale at the vet's office. You can also use targeting for a recall. Once your dog looks at you, you present the target and it serves as their cue to come to you to touch your hand. It is also handy as a calm, relaxed, focus-on-you behavior.

The Hand Target behavior is built in three steps.

1. Start with a closed fist (about 2 inches from the dog's nose) with a yummy, bit of treat inside. Mark (your visual "clicker" or "yes" sign) for his nose touching your fist. Open your fist and let the dog have the food. You can try this in mini sessions throughout the day of 1-3 minutes (or 10-20 repetitions). Be sure that the dog is touching your hand and that you are not touching your hand to the dog's nose.

2. Next, begin with a closed fist (without treat) 2 inches from the dog's nose. As before, mark the second the dog's nose touches your fist. Then, reach for a tiny bit of something yummy (reinforce). Repeat as suggested in step one in mini sessions with multiple repetitions. If the dog does not touch your fist with his nose after 3 seconds remove your fist and then immediately offer it again for another try. If, after 3 tries, the dog does not touch your fist, go back to step one and practice more at this easier level.

3. Step three is using an open palm, deliberate "target" hand. Once more, begin with the target hand about 2 inches from the dog's nose. What we are seeking is a deliberate "nose bump" of your hand. As with previous steps, if the dog does not target your hand in 3 seconds, remove your hand but immediately offer another chance with your hand coming right back out. Also, if after 3 tries the dog does not target your hand with his/her nose, back up to step two and practice.

You'll also want to begin to have your hand on different sides, up a bit, down a little, and then moving (going very slowly and backing up to a previous step if the dog doesn't touch after 3 tries).

In new, or distracting environments, for example with another animal nearby, someone cooking dinner, children running around, or people shouting outside, etc., you may need to back up to an easier step and progress forward. Remember, the goal is to set your dog up to succeed and to make it as easy as possible for them to do so.

An example of a practical use of the hand target would be at the veterinarian's office. Once you have built a reliable hand touch and you would like your dog to move onto the scale you just move your target hand onto the scale and your dog follows to touch with his nose. Then you would mark with your "yes" sign and reinforce with something tasty.

Tylee Pippen, Shiro (Rocket)

Another great default behavior that you will want to cultivate is "checking in." This means that your dog gives a glance back at you. In order for this to become routine and a habit you will want to make it extra reinforcing for your dog. So, be prepared! Have a treat pouch on you with yummy (in your dog's eyes!) bits of something worthwhile and every time your dog looks at you "pay" him for that behavior by giving him a treat! Again, the more that you practice this consistently, the more often your dog will check in. The more behavior is repeated, the stronger it becomes, which is exactly what you are going for!

Generalizing

Once you have practiced hand targeting in a quiet, distraction free environment, you will want to begin to practice in new places. Dogs do not generalize well and as such, you will need to practice in each room of your house, inside and outside, and eventually, in spots along walks, in vet's offices, in shops, and in any other environment that you can think of where your dog may go.

Scott Vinnicombe Photography, Radar

Myths

Deaf Doesn't Equal Difficult

While training your deaf dog may require some modifications, it is not more difficult than committing to training a hearing animal. It can be a fun and enriching process for both you and your deaf pup!

Too, deaf dogs are not "suffering" with their disability, but in fact don't know that they are deaf. As with any dog, your deaf dog needs a clear communication method to educate them about how we would like them to behave while living with us in our environment.

Difference in Learners

Sandee Hutchinson, George

While it is of vital importance to understand the species of learner that you are working with, and to also know the individual, in terms of learning, the concept is the same for all be they earthworm, elephant, human, or deaf dog. According to Ken Ramirez, biologist and animal behaviorist, "Learning is learning. Whether you are teaching a child or working with your spouse or dealing with an employee or dealing with an animal-the laws of learning are a science and if you understand the science of how creatures learn, you can help to take care of them better."

No matter the species, antecedents (triggers) precede behavior. Consequences follow behavior. We can arrange some antecedents and we can control consequences. In this way we can help to shape behavior by understanding how to manipulate antecedents by controlling the consequences, which will either strengthen or weaken the target behavior. The concept is the science based ABC (antecedent, behavior, consequence) applied behavioral analysis approach to learning.

Dominance/Pack Leader

Lindsey Phipps, Lilee

The "alpha" or "pack leader" myth is just that. It is a mentality that has been scientifically proven to be inaccurate and outdated. While showing leadership and compassionately teaching your dog, you don't need to be the "pack leader."

The approach to canine social behavior known as "dominance theory" was based upon original studies that were done with captive wolves in the 1930-40s. The original researcher's observations were then poorly extrapolated to wild wolf behavior and then to domestic dogs.

Later, David Mech stated, "attempting to apply information about the behavior assemblages of unrelated captive wolves to familial structure of natural packs has resulted in considerable confusion." He further states, "the concept of the alpha wolf as 'top dog' ruling a group of similar-aged compatriots is particularly misleading."

This misinformation and misinterpretation later translated to "wolves live in hierarchical packs with a ruling aggressive alpha—dogs descended from wolves—therefore, humans must be dominant over dogs." (Pat Miller, De-Bunking the Alpha Dog Theory)

Fortunately, more recently the science of behavior and learning has begun to be disseminated more widely. Too, advances in positive training and an increasingly educated dog training profession have made great strides.

Unfortunately, in the early 2000's popular culture has made famous television programs, which have put dominancy theory back in fashion. While force and punishment based methods are a piece of the operant conditioning quadrants and have proven for decades that they may work, they come with significant fallout.

Finally, the presumption that dogs would consider us members of their canine pack is preposterous. We co-exist best with other species via peaceful interactions and reliance on communication.

Lee Charles Kelley has compiled the following resources, which demonstrate the disproven Dominance/Alpha/Pack Leader theories:

"Since we have so many television shows, books, and other media which have, unfortunately, not only been perpetuating this faulty view, but basing training and behavior modification methods upon it, it is important that the public be made aware of the real truth of wolf packs." - "The Man Who Cried Alpha," Nicole Wilde.

"Writers who refer to dominance and alpha behavior in dog training are basing their message on outdated and now disproved theory (Steinker, 2007a)." -- The Alpha Theory: based on a misguided premise, Debra Millikan

"It won't be hard to get the wolf pack mentality to go by the board simply because we don't think many of the experts ever really believed it. It is through social play that animals learn from one another. Further, it is fun to play with our dogs even if none of us learn anything. It will certainly make more sense to the dog than to be tumbled onto its back and growled at by a human." -- A Talk with Ray and Lorna Coppinger

"Dominance theory is so muddled that it often contradicts itself. For example, if a 'dominant dog' is acting aggressively and the solution is through 'calm-assertive' energy, which makes the human the 'dominant pack leader,' wouldn't a dominant dog always act calm-assertive instead of aggressive?" -- The Dog Whisperer Controversy, Lisa Mullinax

"The concept of the alpha wolf as a 'top dog' is particularly misleading." - University of Minnesota, Professor L. David Mech

Food as Bribery

Positive reinforcement training is about using what your dog finds reinforcing. Food is a primary reinforcer and your dog has to eat, thus it makes sense to use this tool to our training advantage. Note that this does not equate to deprivation.

Your dog's daily food will not be contingent upon performing behaviors as if they choose not to do as cued, they should still receive their daily food supply (perhaps after the training session in the form of a food puzzle).

Dogs who are bribed SEE the food before the behavior is offered. They quickly learn that it is only rewarding to respond when they can clearly see food present. This is using food as a bribe.

On the other hand, using food as a reinforcer means that the food only appears AFTER a behavior has been performed. In this case the dog learns that good things happen after behaviors; which makes transferring and incorporating non-food reinforcers into the training program possible.

Guilty/Stubborn/Ignoring

We often think that dogs look "guilty" when they respond to facial features and body language. If your dog has done something that you aren't pleased about, rather than guilt, you are likely observing appeasement expressions as he/she reads your face and body language and attempts to provide clues about how they are feeling regarding your anger/frustration.

Similarly, dogs are sometimes thought to be acting, "stubborn" or to be "ignoring" you. Dogs don't have the cognitive ability to conscientiously decide to ignore you or to be stubborn. More likely is that your communication with your dog has not been as clear as you imagine. Even if you feel sure that your dog "understands" and is just not doing as you would like, take a step back. Try re-teaching the behavior. Break it down into smaller pieces and be certain that your reinforcers are of a high enough value.

For example, if your dog is on the couch, they may find the comfortable spot more reinforcing than the tidbit that you are offering for them to come off of the couch and approach you. Try re-training another way and practice, practice, practice. Also, remember that dogs don't generalize well and thus, behaviors need to be practiced in each different area where you are expecting them to be performed. Be mindful of distractions and how they affect your training efforts; be sure to practice with low distractions and then with many distractions.

For example, if your dog looks right at you and then walks off to sniff another dog, he is not ignoring you, nor being stubborn, he simply may not understand your recall cue. It may not have been practiced around such high distraction and otherwise reinforcing exciting things such as another dog. Once more, begin again with tiny steps and practice.

Permissive Training

Using positive reinforcement in our interactions with our deaf dogs is not being permissive, but rather is using clear communication and providing feedback to the animal when they have done something that we like.

According to Dr. Susan Friedman, http://www.behaviorworks.org/files/articles/APDT%20What's%20Wrong%20with%20this%20Picture%20-%20Dogs.pdf, "The commitment to using the most positive, least intrusive, effective interventions allows us to think before we act, so that we make choices about the means by which we accomplish our behavior goals. In this way, we can be both effective and humane."

Training Age

Dogs are always learning, no matter their age. According to Susan Garret, "Nothing is ever trained. Behaviors are constantly getting better or getting worse." Hence, it is best to make use of that fact and use it to your advantage by capturing, reinforcing, and training appropriate behavior that you would like to see increase/continue. By the time that your puppy is seven to eight weeks you can begin socialization or puppy classes.

You have likely heard the term, "socialization." When talking about dogs we are actually referring to the most important, critical period of your dog's life. Up until they are three months old it is vital to allow them to have as many positive experiences as possible with as many sights, sounds, interactions (people and animals), environments and stimuli as possible. Note, that the important factor in this scenario is to have as many *positive* experiences as possible, thus it will be your job to be sure that your puppy isn't overwhelmed or frightened by something, but that you set him/her up for successful opportunities.

It is the position of the American Veterinary Society of Animal Behavior that puppies should be socialized prior to having all of their vaccine series completed (they should, of course be started). They state that the vital importance of socialization to avoid potential fear and aggression issues later in life out weights any possible risks associated with exposing a puppy not fully vaccinated (series of vaccines) to the wide world. http://avsabonline.org/uploads/position_statements/puppy_socialization.pdf According to the AVSAB, "Because the first three months are the period when sociability outweighs fear, this is the primary window of opportunity for puppies to adapt to new people, animals, and experiences.

Incomplete or improper socialization during this important time can increase the risk of behavioral problems later in life including fear, avoidance, and/or aggression. Behavioral problems are the greatest threat to the owner-dog bond. In fact, behavioral problems are the number one cause of relinquishment to shelters. Behavioral issues, not infectious diseases, are the number one cause of death for dogs under three years of age."

On the flip side, the adage that you can't teach an old dog new tricks is also one that has been disproven over and over. As long as your animal is physically capable, they are able to learn at any time.

Frequently Asked Questions

Barking

Natasha Aymami, Marley

If your deaf pup is barking inappropriately, you'll first need to get their attention. You can do this by moving your arms around, gently jingling (not tugging!) the leash, thumping the floor (to make a vibration), turning room lights off/on, or moving yourself to within your dog's vision.

Next, as I've noted before, rather than training a "no" sign, better yet, teach your dog what you DO want them to do and ask for it. If you have a nice "hand target" or "sit" default behavior (a behavior that you have practiced over and over and in many locations) sign your signal for that behavior. If you have practiced the cookie in the hand impulse behavior ("It's Yer Choice" activity by Susan Garrett), put a treat in your hand and wait. Your dog can then decide to continue barking or.... sit, wait, target, etc. (do what you are seeking) in order to have an opportunity to earn something reinforcing. It will be your reinforcement history (practice!) that will help your dog to make a good decision!

Crate Training

Dr. Anna Kilborn, Apollo

Crate training is a valuable and important management tool. Appropriately training your dog to love his crate and to consider it a safe, secure, wonderful spot is a key component to a happy, relaxed home environment.

Step one is to purchase a crate. There are generally three different types of crates.

One, the plastic airline variety (http://www. petsmart.com/dog/crates-gates-containment/grreat-choice-dog-carrier-zid36-531/ cat-36-catid-100013?var_id=36-531&_ t=pfm%3Dcategory). The advantage of this style is that if you may have the need for travel, this crate can double for at home and on the road use.

Two, the metal type, which are generally all metal with a tray at the bottom (http://www.petsmart.com/dog/crates-gates-containment/midwest-life-stages-single-door-folding-dog-crate-zid36-6362/cat-36-catid-100013?var_id=36-6362&_t=pfm%3Dcategory). This type of crate has visibility from all sides, as it is a wire side-top crate.

The final type is a sturdy cloth crate (http://www.petsmart.com/dog/crates-gates-containment/nature-s-miracle-trade-port-a-crate-dog-crate-zid36-7281/cat-36-catid-100013?var_id=36-7281&_t=pfm%3Dcategory). These generally have doors, which close via zippers.

It may be best to train initially with one of the first two types, as they are more "escape proof" and sturdy. In any event, you wouldn't want to leave your dog unattended in a crate where he was not feeling comfortable as you will always want the crate to have a positive association.

Your dog should be able to stand up, preferably sit, turn around, and lie down comfortably inside of their crate. You don't want to have too much additional space beyond what is described above. You will want your dog to understand that this is his/her safe/comfortable spot, however you won't want extra room for toileting. Crates will often have approximate breed or weight descriptions on them to assist with appropriate sizing. Too, if you purchase a crate for the adult size of your dog, you can block off partial access while using it with a smaller puppy.

Next, if you have the type of plastic crate, which comes apart, you should begin with just the bottom (once you have the steps below with only the bottom, add the top and repeat, then add the door and repeat). Otherwise, try to begin with the door off or, at the least, secured "open." Watch for your pup even glancing at the crate, then signal your "marker" and reinforce with a tiny bit of deliciously yummy food. When building this behavior (crating training) you will want to have a rapid rate of reinforcement. This means looking for any tiny reason to mark and reinforce behavior.

Essentially your training may look like this:

- glance in direction of crate CT (CT=click/"yes" signal and treat)
- glance=CT
- step towards crate=CT
- look at crate=CT
- sniff crate=CT
- one food in=CT
- etc., building up to the whole body voluntarily inside of the crate

Remember that learning is not a linear path in an upward direction. That is to say your dog may look at the crate, receive the treat, and then leave the room. It may take you several look at crate=CT (could be many) before you progress to a next step. Be patient! Be consistent. Look for any excuse (any slight interest at all) to CT your dog's crate interest. They'll gradually and naturally come to have a more substantial interest in the crate (moving towards the crate, to a peek inside, to a paw inside). Never push your dog nor force them into the crate. You may toss a few pieces in once you have ALREADY gotten some initial interest, however you will want to avoid creating a "lure." Just tossing food inside as a "lure" has the danger of building a behavior dependent upon the lure. Better to mark and then reinforce to build a strong behavior.

Once your dog is voluntarily going into the crate, continue to reinforce it (positioning your reinforcers at the back of the crate) as an "awesome" place to be. You will want to close the door for just a few seconds at the beginning. You will want to (casually) re-open the door before your dog becomes upset or alarmed. Be sure never to open the door if the dog is crying, barking, or pawing at the door. This will only reinforce these undesirable behaviors. Instead, draw their attention to the rear of the crate where they can respond to a hand (finger) target through the crate and you can mark and reinforce, whilst then uneventfully opening the door. Better yet, open the door before your dog becomes upset in the crate, thus setting your dog up for success!

You'll want to increase the dog's time in the crate very slowly, at first with you in sight, and eventually with you out of sight in small steps. You can also provide your pup with a stuffed KONG or other valuable toy while in the crate to again, create a positive association with being inside.

Crates should never be used as a punishment and should always be maintained to have a happy, association for your dog.

You may want to leave the door off of your dog's crate or secure it open. Leave a comfortable dog bed inside and some yummy treats and allow your dog access. If you happen past and your dog has voluntarily entered their crate, gently toss in a few tiny treats to reinforce this nice behavioral choice.

Counter Surfing

As we've mentioned, dogs (and all learners) will do what is most reinforcing. Often times something of interest is left in plain view/smell on a countertop or table and a dog will attempt to or actually get said object. Prior to this happening, as with all behaviors, we will want to employ a management strategy while training what we DO want the dog to do.

Your system of management should begin before the problem starts. This means that right from when your dog comes through your door for the first time, you are conscious and conscientious about where and what things are on counters and surfaces within reach of your pup.

You have probably heard a variety of suggests for solving this type of problem from signing the word or your signal for "no" to using spray bottles, to having things topple on the dog, to startling them via electronic devices. I

Hear No Evil Australian Deaf Dog Rescue

urge you to use none of these methods as all of them are aversive and/or punishing to some degree they all thus have the ability to come with unwanted side effects (apathy, escape-avoidance, generalized fear, and aggression). They may break down rather than build up your relationship with your animal. As a result, using one of the above methods can actually create new problems.

Instead, I suggest the following. First, as mentioned above, manage the situation while training. Keep counters clear (even of crumbs), food items put away, and things not meant to be explored via doggy mouths safely unavailable. The reason that this first step is so very important is that the adage "practice makes perfect" is true for behaviors that we like as well as those that we don't wish to see repeated. Allowing the dog to have some practice at scarfing items from counters and tables begins to establish this reinforcing behavior, which, is then more difficult to change.

A clever metaphor for this situation is described by Kiki Yablon: If when you went to take out the garbage, you found a $50 bill in the trash can, you might think to look in the can again the next day. If you found another $50 bill in the can you might almost look forward to taking a peek in the bin the next day. If the following day there was nothing, but then a week later, there was another $50 bill, it's likely you may continue checking for a while to come! Basically, all this is to say that if the chance of reinforcement exists (perhaps based upon previous experience), then it's more difficult to convince the dog that some different behavior (not sneaking things off of counters/table tops) is more reinforcing.

Next, you will want to actively work on training other behaviors that you like better (than counter surfing) and that are possibly incompatible (not physically able to be completed at the same time).

Examples of such trainable behaviors are "settle" (teaching your pup to settle on a mat), "sit" (teaching your pup that "sitting" is much more reinforcing than counter surfing), "find it" (on the floor) whereby your pup learns to look for "good things" on the floor (that you have put there) so that he associates the floor and not the counters with yummy/fun items. A qualified professional positive trainer can help with the specifics of teaching these behaviors. It's a well spent investment!

You can also work on impulse control. Susan Garrett's "It's Yer Choice" is a game that helps dogs understand and make good decisions. It begins with you having some treats in your closed hand. Brace your hand on your arm and do NOT move it. Your dog may try to lick, pry, paw it open to get at the treats. Only when your dog backs away(this *will* happen) do you open your hand. As the sight and smell of treats is reinforcing, the dog will likely move toward your hand, at which time you should close your fist (do not move your hand). The dog moves away again and your fist opens again. When your dog can wait calmly with your fist open, treats laying there, and not moving towards the treats, only then will you pick up a treat (again, if the dog moves, put treat back and close fist) and feed it to him. This game practiced over time and expanded to the floor and to "sit," "down" and "stay" cues will help your dog to understand the consequences of his behavior. No access to good things vs. access to good things results in making better decisions. Again, according to Susan Garrett, "You control the resources, and not your dog!"

If you have an "oops" moment and management fails, never run after the dog. A fun game of "chase" is very likely reinforcing and the behavior will then be more apt to be repeated! Instead, run in the other direction or entice your dog to come to you with a "trade up." A "trade up" is something that your dog will consider "better value" than what he's currently got in his mouth. On this note, you never want to just "take" something away from your dog, but rather, you always want to do a trade up to exchange something that the dog has and that you want. Too, trade ups must have a bigger value for the dog than the item that he's currently in position of, so keep track of what your dog considers a "big value" treat!

Finally, always remember that behaviors that are reinforced will become stronger and be repeated. So, if you notice your dog sitting or relaxing nicely, be sure to reinforce that behavior! Toss some favorite treats their way. Don't wait until your dog does something that you don't like, but rather, watch for ways that you can "catch" your dog doing something that you do like and reinforce it in a big way!

Food

Karen Lawe, Gollum

While you certainly can feed your dog from a bowl, it is a lost opportunity, as mentioned before. Prior to domestication, dogs spent sixty percent of their time seeking food! Now, however, feeding from a plate or a bowl eliminates that instinct. Instead, use a food puzzle, like a KONG (http://www.aspca.org/pet-care/virtual-pet-behaviorist/dog-behavior/

how-stuff-kong-toy) or Wobbler (http://www.amazon.com/KONG-Wobbler-Treat-Dispensing-Large/dp/B003ALMW0M), or a food puzzle ball (http://www.amazon.com/Omega-Paw-Tricky-Treat-Large/dp/B0002DK26M/ref=cm_lmf_tit_4).

These options allow your dog to have mental stimulation while eating. You can also create some DIY options; however, as with any food puzzle, dogs should never be left unsupervised. Some homemade options may include kibble inside of an empty gallon water jug with the top off. To make this option easier, you can also cut one or more holes in the side of the bottle. Using an empty plastic peanut butter jar with kibble inside and the lid off works well, too. A muffin tin with some food placed in a few of the tins and covered (all slots) with tennis balls will engage your dog's mind!

The scientific explanation for the phenomenon of animals preferring to work for their food is called, "contra freeloading." You'll sometimes see folks say that we are making animals "work" for food, which they believe, isn't kind. In fact, the opposite is true. Contra freeloading indicates that even if food is readily available in abundance, animals will often choose to obtain food via operant conditioning such as pushing a lever to get food. Accordingly, it has been concluded that "working" for food allows animals to gather information about their ever-changing environments.

Jumping

Jodie Spady, Pippin

You will often hear people respond to this issue with one or several of the following suggestions: knee to chest, teach sign for "no" or "off" (both corrections *after* the behavior has taken place), or put your hand up to stop.

When a dog is jumping up they are likely seeking attention. As such, any physical contact, signing, or verbal (even though they cannot hear, they are very perceptive with body language, which will include facial expressions) attention is actually reinforcing this behavior.

Remember, your dog does not need correction. They need education. Thus, teach them that jumping earns nothing. The moment that the dog has four paws back on the ground, use your sign for "yes!" and reinforce with something your dog really enjoys. A level 10 reinforcer would be appropriate here as you are competing with the urge to jump for attention, thus you need to make it more reinforcing to have all paws on the floor.

"No!"

Wendy Gordon & Daniel Korn, Bonnie

The word, and in the case of deaf dogs, the signal or sign for "no" is something that I do not suggest using valuable training time on. Telling an animal "no" does not in fact provide much information. It is not a very clear communication tool as it leaves the situation rather nebulous as in "No what?" Instead, I strongly recommend working on incompatible behaviors and impulse control training so that you can teach your dog and give him/her the choice to make good decisions about what you DO want them to do!

Hearing vs Deaf

Much of appropriate dog training will be the same for a hearing or a deaf dog, with obvious visual adaptations. As such, if you are training a deaf dog along with a hearing dog both dogs can be trained the same way. I would suggest doing some training on specifics separately so that your timing for marking (and then reinforcing) can be spot on with each dog. This would hold true any time that you are working with multiple animals. However, once you are well on your way with a specific behavior you can work with both dogs together. I use a visual "hand flash" marker as my deaf dog clicker and use a clicker or verbal marker ("yes!") with my hearing dogs, however they all know hand signals as well.

Greta Salem, Duncan

Obsessive Compulsive Disorder (ODC)

When folks discuss OCD they are actually talking about fearful responses to triggers. A trigger is the sudden appearance of something that happens before a behavior. Triggers are also called antecedents. Triggers can be something that the dog sees, smells, or hears (in the case of hearing dogs), or perceives. For example, a bicycle or man wearing a hat can be triggers.

Triggers or antecedents are followed by behaviors. An example is if you were to cue your dog to "sit." When your dog sits you would reinforce their "sit" with a treat. In this scenario, the cue for "sit" is the trigger/antecedent, the "sit" is the behavior, and the treat is the consequence. It's easy to remember when you think of it in terms of A-B-C (antecedent-behavior-consequence)!

Introductions

Dogs

Lindsey Phipps, Lilee

Introducing your deaf dog to other canines should ideally always be done on neutral ground. Relaxed, calm handlers should have each dog on leash. Leashes should be kept loose, as tension on leashes might communicate to the dog that you are feeling anxious. Begin by walking the dogs side by side at a safe distance and then allow the dogs to sniff where the other has walked.

The next step would be to allow the dogs to approach each other while still on loose leashes. Keeping a keen eye on the dog's body language and paying attention to their interactions is important. You will be watching for loose, wiggly bodies. Sniffing end to end (rather than nose to nose) is appropriate. Take care not to allow a hearing dog to accidentally "sneak" up behind and startle your deaf pup.

If introducing the dogs to the same household, putting away any food, bowls, or toys ahead of time will avoid any potential conflicts.

Allow the dogs to take frequent breaks from each other and if you are uncomfortable at any time, please consult a professional trainer who is knowledgeable about dog body language.

People

When meeting new people, your deaf dog might feel most comfortable if they are the ones making the advances. Ask folks to allow your dog to approach and sniff without making any movements (this includes hands) towards your deaf dog. When the situation is in the dog's control they can feel more confident and comfortable. Reinforce calm behavior. You may want to set your dog up for success by having him leashed (even inside the house) without tension on the lead.

Kathi Hiatt, Odd Otis

Kathi Hiatt, Odd Otis

Do not force introductions and keep them brief and positive. Again, reinforce your dog (mark and treat) for appropriate behavior that you would like to see repeated.

If your dog is fearful of people, a protocol of desensitization and counter conditioning (DS/CC) is recommended. This means that you'll use a combination of asking for behaviors in the presence of the trigger and marking and reinforcing as well as just providing treats while the trigger (scary person) is within range.

In this way we work to change the dog's conditioned emotional response (CER) from "person=scary" to "person=good things!" The following link provides a more in depth explanation of DS/CC. http://www.training-your-dog-and-you.com/Desensitizing_and_counter-conditioning.html

House Training

House training is one of the biggest hurdles that new puppy/dog families experience. However, the solution is not complicated, nor difficult. It only requires patience and consistency. The amount of time house training will take will depend on your efforts and consistency and the dog's history (of not being properly taught where it is acceptable to toilet).

First, crate training (see above) is highly recommended. Crate training can aid in management and sets your dog up for success. Your dog should be crated whenever they are not able to be 100% supervised until you are reliably confident and trust in their appropriate behavior. Keep in mind that puppies under six months and older dogs who are not

Hear No Evil Australian
Deaf Dog Rescue

yet house trained should not be crated for more than three or four hours at a time (that means initially getting up to take them outside to use the bathroom during the night).

When you take your dog out of their crate you should go immediately outside with them leashed. Then stand in one spot. Do not walk around. Often times folks like to "walk the dog" and then at the end when the dog does their business they whisk them back indoors. In the dog's mind, when they go to the bathroom, the fun ends. Thus, they may want to prolong toileting. While standing in the one spot when your dog goes to the bathroom you can "label" the behavior with a sign for "bathroom" if you like. Do not make the sign for "bathroom" before they go as they haven't yet made the connection and won't know what you are intending to communicate. If you do choose to implement a "bathroom" sign, eventually, once your dog DOES understand the concept, you can use it just like any other cue to get your dog to do the behavior-in this case going to the bathroom!

Once your dog finishes-the very second they are done-have a "praise party!" Give your dog love and snuggles and give your sign for "good!" Then, take them for a little walk around or allow some playtime before heading back inside.

If, your dog does not go to the bathroom after standing in one spot for a few minutes, take them back inside and re-crate. Try taking them back out in another 5-10 minutes and repeat the above sequence.

Inside, when not crated or 100% (this does mean eyes on your dog as you are watching or actively engaged with him/her) supervised, they should be "tethered" to you. You can use their leash and attach it to a belt or if longer, around your waist. Again, you are helping your dog to succeed and not allowing them to get into situations where they may fail.

If, while tethered to you your puppy begins to squat or otherwise start to go to the bathroom, interrupt with a "surprise" look (very important that you don't show anger or frustration towards the dog as it will associate WHAT not WHERE as the issue), and scoop/scoot them quickly outside. Once outside, stand in your spot and if they finish, again have your "praise party!" If there is nothing more, head back indoors and tether or crate and try for another outside bathroom break in 20-30 minutes.

Lastly, if your pup has an accident in the house it is always the fault of the caregiver. This message bears repeating, as it is a failure on your part to effectively communicate to your pup. Your dog's behavior is NEVER wrong. Watch for your puppy sniffing or circling. If there is an accident and you haven't caught the dog in the act (and interrupted neutrally to rush outside to finish, without anger, mind you), just clean it up (preferably with some odor neutralizing pet spray designed specifically for this type of event). Make a note to be ever more vigilant about observing your dog and watching for body language so as to get your pup outside in time to go and then have the opportunity to praise them for a job well done!

The toilet training may seem tedious, however, the more consistently you implement the above, the faster it will all go, and the sooner you will have a house trained dog!

Resources

Ash Bowler, Buzz

The following links provide searches via zip code and/ or country for positive reinforcement trainers locally. When a new dog joins your family, it is always a great idea and bonding experience to take a couple of lessons with a qualified professional who can help you to communicate more effectively with your new deaf dog friend thus avoiding frustration and confusion. The investment that you might make will help to set you all up for a lifetime of success!

http://www.petprofessional-guild.com/PetGuildMembers

https://www.karenpryoracademy.com/find-a-trainer

As a final thought, please remember that the animal is never wrong. Everything that the animal does is because it is in some way reinforcing to them. Therefore, if confusion is present, remain calm, re-think your communication strategy, and implement a plan which, rather than punishes, reinforces behavior. This is the win/win solution for a happier, healthier environment for your deaf dog and their human family!

Made in the USA
Lexington, KY
04 July 2019